CHILD *of the* LIGHT

CHILD *of the* LIGHT

WALKING THROUGH ADVENT & CHRISTMAS

Beth A. Richardson

UPPER
ROOM BOOKS®
NASHVILLE

CHILD OF THE LIGHT
Walking through Advent and Christmas
© 2005 by Beth A. Richardson
All rights reserved.

The Upper Room® Web site: http://www.upperroom.org

Unless otherwise noted, scripture quotations are from the New
Revised Standard Version Bible, copyright 1989 Division of Christian
Education of the National Council of the Churches of Christ in the
United States of America. Used by permission. All rights reserved.

"I Want to Walk as a Child of the Light" by Kathleen Thomerson.
Copyright © 1970, 1975 Celebration. Used by permission.

Excerpts from "O Come, O Come, Emmanuel" St. 1, refrain, 7ab
Copyright © 1940, 1943, renewed 1981 by The Church Pension Fund.
Used by permission of Church Publishing, New York, NY.

Cover design: TMW Designs
Cover image: SuperStock
Interior design: Nancy Terzian / nterdesign.com
First printing: 2005

LIBRARY OF CONGRESS CATALOGING IN PUBLICATION DATA
Richardson, Beth A.
   Child of the light : walking through Advent and Christmas / Beth
A. Richardson.
      p. cm.
   ISBN 0-8358-9816-4
   1. Advent. 2. Christmas.   I. Title.
BV40.R52 2005
242'.33--dc22   2005011649

Printed in the United States of America

To my mother and father,
Margaret and Charles Richardson,
who taught me to love music, liturgy, and Advent

CONTENTS

A COMING into BEING

The Christmas season—the high point of the year for many people around the world. The preparation for Christmas, the decorating, the celebrations, the music and worship observances, the giving of gifts and gathering of families—all these rituals mark this important event in the life of our faith.

Often during this time of year I find myself saying, "It can't be December!" or "It doesn't feel like it's time to get ready for Christmas." My insides are not ready for this—the increased stress, the traffic jams, the crowds, the frantic feeling that I can't get it all done or that I'm going to forget something or someone important. The demands of the culture and of my own expectations overwhelm me at a time when I want to be more and more focused on God and the sacred events of Christmas.

I guess that's why I really like Advent, the season of the church year preceding Christmas. Advent, liturgically speaking, includes the four Sundays before Christmas during which we Christians prepare our hearts, minds, and spirits for the Advent, the birth, of the Christ child.

Webster's Dictionary defines the word *advent* as "a coming into being" (Merriam-Webster's *Collegiate® Dictionary*, Tenth Edition). "A coming into being." That's what I'm in need of right now. I need this time of Advent to bring me into being. I need to slow down, to live in the moment, to appreciate the small things—the warmth and light of a candle flame, the tiny fingers of a newborn baby, the quiet stillness of the dawn, the enthusiastic smiles of children. I need to prepare my heart, to make my spirit ready for the birth of the Messiah.

We all need this time of Advent to slow us down, to open our ears to God's quiet voice, to guide us through the chaos of the consumerist culture that Christmas has become. As we make our way through this busy season, let us allow God to shape our minds and hearts—to become a part of God's "coming into being" in Jesus' birth.

TAKE TIME FOR GOD

The thought of adding space for spiritual reflection during the Advent season often seems overwhelming. Personally and culturally this time of year already seems to race out of control toward a Christmas finish line. There are so many tasks that need to be done, so many expectations to meet. How could I possibly add one more thing to my life?

During this time of year the pace of life speeds up. We rush around trying to buy the perfect gifts, throw the best party, prepare a spotless home for holiday guests, and write the most excellent Christmas letter to be mailed in time to arrive before the Blessed Event. During this chaotic season, we are invited to take time to prepare ourselves spiritually for the coming of the Christ child. That's what Advent is all about—preparing our hearts and minds and spirits for God's coming.

Take time? That's a ridiculous suggestion! I hardly have time to do what needs to get done before the family comes to my house for Christmas! Time is the one thing I don't have! And when I try meditation or prayer, I'm thinking and worrying about what I should be doing instead. The silence overflows with anxious thoughts. I figure it would be better to just go back to my to-do list, so at least something is being accomplished.

Take time for God: that's exactly the challenge God gives us during this season of preparation. In Advent, we are invited to take time out from our busyness to be with God. We make time for meditation, prayer, scripture study, or journaling. And in doing so, we nurture our spiritual self, that sometimes fragile part of us who longs for a connection with God.

I believe that even in our frantic culture, in our busy lives, and during this hectic season of the year, we can learn to spend time with God. Regular people like us, not just "spiritual superstars," can accomplish setting aside a little time each day to prepare our hearts for the coming of the Christ child.

USING THIS RESOURCE

Whether reading this book in relationship with others (church group, covenant group, choir group, or family) or alone, I hope *Child of the Light* will help us think each day about how God is present in our lives. Regard this resource as a sort of Advent Survival Guide, providing times of spiritual nurture when it is most needed, during this season before Christmas. And don't forget that Christmas does not end on December 25. The season of Christmas stretches for twelve days, concluding on Epiphany, January 6. We will continue reading this book beyond Advent and all the way to Epiphany.

Each of the first four chapters draws its theme from a different Advent hymn or carol. Once we reach Christmas, meditations feature a number of different Christmas hymns or carols. Each day of the week offers a hymn text along with a scripture reading, reflection, and a prayer.

Try to take at least ten minutes each day for time with God. Many people find it helpful to set aside the same time every day. Think about when you can be alone and relatively quiet. It could be first thing in the morning or late in the evening. Give some attention to the physical space for your quiet time. Create a simple worship center or quiet space in your home. Put out a small crèche, candle, or Advent wreath as a reminder of the season. Carve out a certain time each day for prayer and meditation. Put the quiet time on your calendar or day planner. Honor your inner self by keeping that appointment with God each day. At the appointed time, light a candle or put on some special music. (If possible, play the Advent hymn for that week's meditations.)

Seeing the birds or other wildlife may help you connect with God. Try having spiritual time near a window in view of bird feeders or garden wildlife. Turn off the radio and the television. Resolve not to answer the phone or check e-mail during these scheduled minutes. (That recommendation may seem self-evident, but many of us forget that it's counterproductive to multitask devotional time.) This is your time for God. And the fruits of this time are many—centeredness, assurance, connection with God, and the feeling and knowledge that you are loved and cared for by God.

Each Sunday during Advent, consider creating an Advent worship time for the family. Light the candles on the Advent wreath. Use the first reading of each chapter as the liturgy for this lighting. If there are children, lighting the Advent wreath can be an especially meaningful family worship experience. (Check Upper Room Ministries' *Pockets* magazine or its Web site—www.pockets.org—to find family rituals for lighting the candles of the Advent wreath.)

Since Christmas falls on different days of the week, you may not need all the meditations for the fourth week of Advent. Read each day's meditation through December 23, then turn to the page for Christmas Eve, page 79, and move forward from there.

ABOUT THE MUSIC

Some readers might be wondering about these particular Advent hymn choices: *Where are "Joy to the World" or "Angels We Have Heard on High"? We've been seeing Christmas decorations and hearing Christmas songs or hymns in the stores since Thanksgiving. Why not use the familiar hymns we like to sing at Christmastime?*

The themes for the first four weeks of *Child of the Light* are inspired by Advent hymns. We're in a time of waiting. We are waiting for the coming of the Christ. We use hymns and carols that reflect these themes of preparation and "not yet." Each week focuses on a different Advent hymn or carol. The themes of the meditations for that week are taken from that particular song.

Sing the hymns during daily quiet time. If a hymn is unfamiliar, try learning the song. Sing the hymn aloud or sing it in your heart. Carry it with you in your heart every day for the week. Play a recording of the hymn each day as a part of your devotional time. If using this book with a group, sing the hymn as a part of group worship time or play a recording of it.

If the hymn is not familiar to you, look for recordings of the it on Christmas CDs. Or you could do an Internet search using the hymn title. You should be able to find a recording of the hymn or hymn tune.

For the Nonmusical

Don't be intimidated if you are unfamiliar with the tune or if singing is not your strength. The words themselves are beautiful poetry and full of rich meaning. Read the text of the hymn and reflect on the words.

Using This Book with Others

It's often easier to keep up a spiritual discipline when we have others to talk with about our experience. In such a situation we can offer one another mutual support. If *Child of the Light* will be used as part of an Advent study offered by a church or covenant group, leaders can follow the suggestions for group use at the end of the book.

If no formal group setting exists, consider inviting one or two other persons to read this book during Advent. Meet weekly at a home or a coffee shop and talk about what each is experiencing through reading and meditation and through daily living. Check out the Group Study Guide at the end of the book. Or just covenant together to read the book and meet regularly during this Advent season.

If no one in a group sings or knows the hymn, read the poetry responsively. Let the words of the hymn help set the context for group discussion and reflection time.

COME,
Thou Long-Expected JESUS

Come, thou long-expected Jesus,
born to set thy people free;
from our fears and sins release us,
let us find our rest in thee.
Israel's strength and consolation,
hope of all the earth thou art;
dear desire of every nation,
joy of every longing heart.

Words: Charles Wesley, 1744
Music: Rowland H. Prichard, 1830

Charles Wesley wrote the lyrics to "Come, Thou Long-Expected Jesus" in 1744. Charles Wesley, born in Lincolnshire, England in 1707, wrote over six thousand hymns during his lifetime. He and his brother John Wesley founded the Methodist movement in the early 1700s. It is said that while John was the organizer, Charles set the theology of the Methodist movement through his abundant hymn texts.

The hymn tune "Hyfrydol" was written by Rowland H. Prichard in 1830. Prichard, a choir director and singer, was from Craienyn, North Wales.

SUNDAY

Song-Prayer

Start out by listening to, singing, or reading meditatively the first stanza of "Come, Thou Long-Expected Jesus." Spend some moments in silence and let the words and the music enter your mind and heart. What word or phrase invites attention?

Read through or listen to the stanza again. This time, listen to what the hymn says to you today. Is there a message you are hearing for the first time? What is God saying through this tune or these words?

Pray the song-prayer that follows on the next page. Sing or read the lines to the song, followed by the prayer. (If listening to a recording of the song, play the section indicated and then pause.) Spend a moment in silence, and then continue to the next phrase.

If you feel led, write a song-prayer and record it in your journal. Close this meditation time by singing or reading the hymn again.

Come, thou long-expected Jesus,
born to set thy people free;

Jesus, Child of God, we welcome you now. Long have we waited for you. Our cluttered minds and our fettered hearts yearn for the freedom you bring.

(Silence)

from our fears and sins release us,
let us find our rest in thee.

Jesus, Child of God, release us from the barriers that keep us from hearing your voice in our world today. Slow down our frantic, busy minds and activities so that we can "find our rest in you."

(Silence)

Israel's strength and consolation,
hope of all the earth thou art;

Jesus, Child of God, you are our strength, our hope, our comfort, and our consolation. You are, indeed, the hope of the world. Send your strength and healing to every broken place, every despondent heart.

(Silence)

dear desire of every nation,
joy of every longing heart.

Jesus, Child of God, you are our desire, our joy, our hunger, our longing. Even nations desire you. We desire your peace and your presence in our hungering world and our longing hearts. Jesus, Child of God, let us welcome you with holy hospitality during this season of Advent. May we prepare a place within our hearts and our lives for your loving presence. Amen.

MONDAY
Advent Hospitality

Come, thou long-expected Jesus.

Come—a command, a verb, a word of invitation, a welcoming. This word of hospitality begins the Advent journey. During Advent, we prepare to welcome a long-awaited, special guest into our lives and our hearts. How do we prepare ourselves for the arrival of God's Child, the Christ? Just as we shop for gifts, clean our homes, rehearse for choir concerts, plan special worship services, prepare seasonal food for our annual celebrations, Advent invites us to prepare our hearts. Advent calls us to sweep out the corners of our heart, to clear away the clutter in our minds and spirits, to make room for the coming of Jesus.

This inner preparation presents us with one of the great challenges of this season. I often wonder, *How could I possibly fit one more thing into this crazy, hectic life of mine? How in the world am I supposed to make time for prayer, meditation, and spiritual preparation?*

But we experience the great paradox of the spiritual life when we enter God's time through prayer, meditation, and study because we are no longer in *chronos* (clock time) but in *kairos* (God time). God time differs from clock time. Entering God time is like taking a journey into a space-time continuum. We're somehow not subject to the same rules of clocks. We gain a life focus; a peace; a loving, connected place that assists us when we reenter clock time. I'm not saying that it will add hours—or even minutes—to our day, but it does change time. Or at least it changes us.

Try these suggestions for engaging in the discipline of preparation and Advent hospitality.

SIMPLICITY

During these weeks when forces all around seem to accelerate, try slowing down the parts of life that you can control. Don't forget to observe a daily ritual of meditation and quiet. When scheduling parties, appointments, and engagements, ask whether you are giving yourself and your family enough time to keep a healthy balance in life. It is okay to say no to invitations or commitments. Seek balance and give yourself and your family or friends the gift of your presence.

Remember to keep Christ at the heart of this season. Resolve to make choices based on this priority.

SEEING GOD IN THE ORDINARY

Practice the spiritual discipline of looking for God in unexpected places. Watch for the presence of God in all that goes on around you. You might see God in an interaction at work, in the words of a stranger, in the face of a child, in the background music at a shopping center.

Watch closely for God as you go through your day. Consider recording in a journal the many ways you experience God's presence. Spend a few moments each evening reflecting on the places where you saw God during the course of the day's activities and interactions.

REFLECTION

For the next week, keep before you the practices of simplicity and seeing God in the ordinary. At the end of the week, reflect on whether or how this awareness affected you.

PRAYER

God of Hospitality, I want to prepare my heart for your coming. Stay close by me as I walk through busy days. Open my eyes and ears and heart that I may see you all around me. Amen.

TUESDAY
One Who Sets Us Free

Come, thou long-expected Jesus,
born to set thy people free.

During Advent we welcome One who was "born to set thy people free." What words of grace—*born to set us free.*

We are in bondage today to so many things. We are held captive by expectations—to do the best, to have the most, to be the happiest, to know the right thing always to say and do and be. We are bound by expectations—from others, of ourselves.

Held captive by our status in life, by possessions, we feel that we must make decisions not just for today but also for retirement, for a spouse's security, for the future of real or anticipated children or grandchildren. We don't travel light like Jesus did. We have possessions to take care of and protect, worldly responsibilities that demand priority in our lives.

Jesus said, "Do not worry about your life, what you will eat or what you will drink, or about your body, what you will wear. Is not life more than food, and the body more than clothing?" (Matt. 6:25). But we do worry. We worry about the past, what we did, what people thought of us, mistakes we made, old hurts we experienced or inflicted upon others. We worry about the future, what we will do or say, how we will cope. We worry about job, family, church, and spiritual life. We are bound by worry.

The God of the captives sent Jesus to set us free from our captivity. Christ frees us from expectations and worry, from the bondage of status and possessions. God calls us to be fully present in the only time we have—in this moment. Let us turn our expectations and worries into prayers to God. Let us release our status and possessions, for God, the source of all, has provided these things for us.

Set me free, Loving God, so that I may better serve you, so that I may better show your love through my words and deeds and actions, that my life might be a reflection of your power and grace and love in the world. Amen.

REFLECTION

Let worries be a reminder of God today. If you are worrying about something, stop and say a prayer, offering the worry to God.

PRAYER

God, I offer [name your worry] to you. May you be present in this worry and in my life this moment. Set me free from my captivity. In your name I pray. Amen.

WEDNESDAY
One Who Frees Us from Fear

From our fears and sins release us,
let us find our rest in thee.

We welcome the One who frees us from fear. What a statement of faith in this day of terrorism! In our post-9/11 world we are captives to fear. We cannot know when or where disaster will strike. Scary people in this world intend to harm ordinary people like us. Underneath my usually confident, adult self, a frightened child longs to be assured that "everything is going to be okay."

To us in our fear and dread Christ comes with words of comfort and strength. Throughout the Advent scriptures we find a message that we are to be set free from fear. Over and over again, we read the words, "Do not be afraid."

When the angel Gabriel appeared, Zechariah "was terrified; and fear overwhelmed him. But the angel said to him, 'Do not be afraid, Zechariah, for your prayer has been heard. Your wife Elizabeth will bear you a son, and you will name him John'" (Luke 1:12-13).

"Do not be afraid to take Mary as your wife," the angel of the Lord said to Joseph in a dream, "for the child conceived in her is from the Holy Spirit" (Matt. 1:20).

The angel Gabriel visited Mary and said to her, "Do not be afraid, Mary, for you have found favor with God. And now, you will conceive in your womb and bear a son, and you will name him Jesus" (Luke 1:30-31).

And Jesus, in his ministry, came to fearful people, saying, "Even the hairs of your head are numbered. Do not be afraid" (Luke 12:7). "Do not let your hearts be troubled, and do not let them be afraid" (John 14:27). "Take heart, it is I; do not be afraid" (Matt. 14:27).

This message of assurance comes to us today, in our uncertain world. Christ says to us, "Do not be afraid, for I am with you. I am walking with you every step you take. No matter what happens, I will be there with you. Trust in me. Trust in my love and my comfort. You do not have to be afraid today."

Take with you today this message of trust: "Do not be afraid."

REFLECTION

What are you afraid of today? As you identify each fear, turn it over to God. "God of courage, I give you this fear of mine, [name the fear]. Replace my fear with trust, my uncertainty with courage. Amen."

PRAYER

"Do not be afraid," the angel said,
over and over again,
to Mary and Joseph, to Zechariah and Elizabeth,
to the shepherds, to anyone who would listen.
"Do not be afraid."
I take these words into my fearful heart
and let them wash over my anxious spirit.
"Do not be afraid."
And I slowly, tentatively reach out my hand
to grasp on to God's promise.
I am not afraid . . . anymore.
Thanks be to God.
Amen.

THURSDAY

One Who Gives Us Rest

Let us find our rest in thee.

We welcome a God in whom we can find rest. These hopeful words comfort us during a season when we seem to be always rushing, always busy, always tired.

God calls us to rest, to take sabbath time in order to re-create our spirits when they have become weary. Even God, the Almighty, took time to rest after creating the heavens and the earth. "On the seventh day God finished the work that [God] had done, and . . . rested on the seventh day. . . . So God blessed the seventh day and hallowed it, because on it God rested from all the work that [God] had done in creation" (Gen. 2:2-3). Sabbath time does not have to be limited to one day of the week. We can choose to weave special sabbath time throughout the week.

Who am I to say that I don't need rest, that I can keep adding activities and commitments to my calendar and tasks to my task list? I am increasingly alarmed by the stimulation of today's electronic world, by the fact that I rarely have time apart, disconnected from my cell phone or my e-mail. I am available 24/7 to the demands of the world. No wonder I am weary and overwhelmed!

Weekends, including Sunday, are the time to catch up on home and family tasks. The laundry needs washing; the house needs cleaning. I have to remember to schedule time for family and friends. If I lead in worship on Sunday morning, it seems more like work than spiritual rest or renewal.

When I do find myself disconnected from electronic communication, I am anxious about being unavailable. *What if someone needs me?* I wonder. It's as if the world revolves around me and might fall apart if I'm not available to help. (It sounds like I think I'm supposed to be God or something.)

We welcome a God in whom we can find rest. A God who gently calls us to a countercultural practice—disconnect. God calls us to take time apart, to turn off the cell phone (not just put it on silent mode), to avoid checking e-mail, and to rest in God. Slow down. Sit. Rest. Empty oneself. Listen. Stop multitasking. Concentrate on the one true thing—God.

Jesus the teacher says to us, "Come to me, all you that are weary and are carrying heavy burdens, and I will give you rest. Take my yoke upon you, and learn from me; for

I am gentle and humble in heart, and you will find rest for your souls. For my yoke is easy, and my burden is light" (Matt. 11:28-30).

REFLECTION

Today take thirty minutes of "unplugged" time. Turn off the cell phone and pager, walk away from the computer and the desk phone. Rest in God. Reflect on this question: *God, what are you saying to me today?*

At the end of the thirty minutes, evaluate what you have experienced during this time. Was it difficult? easy? Is this a spiritual discipline to add to your daily life? What would it take to begin to include this discipline regularly?

Assess sabbath time during the past and coming week. What times of rest do you normally take? What periods of rest do you need to add to life? If you perceive a deficiency of sabbath time, create a plan for change.

Share the plan with one other person—a spouse or friend, a pastor or spiritual director. Ask this person to support this new habit of sabbath time through prayer or periodic check-ins. If you need help in other ways to achieve the goals, share those requests with this person.

PRAYER

Loving God, today may I find my rest in you. Amen.

FRIDAY

One Who Comforts Us

Israel's strength and consolation.

Israel's strength and consolation is also ours. Christ comes to offer us strength and comfort for whatever challenges we face. This phrase in the hymn refers to the coming of the Christ as prophesied in Isaiah.

> Comfort, O comfort my people,
>> says your God.
>
> . . . .
>
> A voice cries out:
> "In the wilderness prepare the way of the LORD,
>> make straight in the desert a highway for our God.
> Every valley shall be lifted up,
>> and every mountain and hill be made low;
> the uneven ground shall become level,
>> and the rough places a plain.
> Then the glory of the LORD shall be revealed,
>> and all people shall see it together,
>> for the mouth of the LORD has spoken.
> (Isa. 40:1, 3-5)

Jesus the tiny baby of the manger is also the Messiah, the Christ who was prophesied from old. In Christ, "the glory of the Lord shall be revealed." We are honored to welcome this Messiah into our homes and into our lives.

When Mary and Joseph take the infant Jesus to Jerusalem to be presented to the Lord, we meet Simeon, a "righteous and devout [man], looking for the consolation of Israel" (Luke 2:25). It had been revealed to Simeon by the Holy Spirit that he would not die until he had seen the Messiah. The Spirit prompts him to go to the Temple that day. When he sees Jesus, he takes the child in his arms and prays to God,

> Master, now you are dismissing your servant in peace,
>> according to your word;
> for my eyes have seen your salvation,
>> which you have prepared in the presence of
>> all peoples,
> a light for revelation to the Gentiles
>> and for glory to your people Israel. (Luke 2:29-32)

Jesus' parents must have been astounded to hear these words about their child. These words invite us to a place of wonder—God has sent this Holy Child, a Messiah and Savior, to people like us! We are called by Advent hospitality to create a place in our lives for his coming.

And not only do we prepare a place for this coming and this child, but a Messiah, a Savior, comes to offer us strength and comfort for all the difficult things we face in our lives. It's like having a houseguest who not only helps with the dishes but also can fix any broken things—physical or spiritual—during his stay.

With honor we anticipate his coming!

REFLECTION

In what places do you need God's strength or comfort? in your family or community? in your church? in the world? Make a list of needs for self, family, community, church, and world.

PRAYER

God, the source of our strength and our comfort, I offer these prayers to you. You are the Comforter, the Sustainer. Be present in all the broken places in my life and in the world. Help me to prepare a place for you this day. Amen.

———◆◆◆◆———

SATURDAY
Practicing Radical Hospitality

———◆◆◆◆———

Hope of all the earth thou art.

We welcome Christ. But Christ calls us to welcome others. Christ, the hope of the earth, invites us to join in a ministry of hospitality.

At my church there's a tradition we follow when we share in our weekly ritual of Holy Communion. We gather, holding hands, in a big circle around the room. On a table in the center of the room wait the bread and the cup of juice. The pastor stands at the table to pray the prayers that consecrate the elements of bread and wine. But before beginning the prayers, the pastor says something like this, "Christ invites you to this table. This table doesn't belong to the pastor. This table doesn't belong to our congregation or to The United Methodist Church. This is the table where Christ is the host. And everyone has a place at this table." And we all repeat, "Everyone has a place at this table."

Around the circle I see people of different ages, races, income levels, physical abilities. I see single people and couples—both gay and straight. I see people from different countries and people with different political perspectives. When I look around the circle, I think of the banquet Jesus talks about in Luke 14:12-13: "When you give a luncheon or a dinner, do not invite your friends or your brothers or your relatives or rich neighbors, in case they may invite you in return, and you would be repaid. But when you give a banquet, invite the poor, the crippled, the lame, and the blind."

When we celebrate Communion together, it reminds us of our ministry of hospitality. We say in our words that all people are welcome, no matter who they are or where they come from. Everyone has a place at the table of Christ.

We live out that ministry of hospitality throughout the week. In the same room where our congregation breaks the Communion bread, we serve lunch to over one hundred hungry people on Tuesdays and Fridays. Every day during the school year, we host a tutoring program for neighborhood children. Volunteers pair up with neighborhood children to work on reading and math. The children have a safe, loving, and fun place to go after school. On Tuesday nights from November through March, twelve homeless people spend the night there. That hospitality is part of a citywide program called Room in the Inn, in which local churches provide a warm place for people to sleep.

The spiritual practice of radical hospitality takes all of us out of our comfort zone. The guest list to my banquets usually includes only people like me. What would it be like to include the stranger, the poor, the crippled, the lame, and the blind of today? What might we be called to do that will push us just a little bit closer to Christ's ministry of hospitality? volunteer in a soup kitchen? tutor a child? help deliver Meals on Wheels to the elderly? visit someone in prison?

Someone once told me that when we arrive at that great heavenly banquet hosted by Christ, we may be surprised by whom we see there. We may think, *Uh-oh! I didn't know that* [fill in the blank here] *would be invited!* Who might you be surprised to see in heaven? an enemy? a Republican? a Democrat? a Muslim? a liberal? a gay or lesbian person? Participating in radical hospitality gives us a head start on that heavenly banquet. We bring the heavenly banquet here to earth, declaring that at the table where Christ is the host, "Everyone has a place at this table."

REFLECTION

How is God calling you to participate in Advent hospitality? Such a call might feel a bit uncomfortable—out of your comfort zone. If you feel an uncomfortable nudge, it may be God's invitation to participate in radical hospitality.

Identify one new way to engage in radical hospitality. To honor Christ's gift to the world, identify one act of hospitality in which to participate before Christmas. Share this commitment with a trusted friend or covenant group.

PRAYER

God of the manger, a gift of hospitality gave you space to be born among animals in a stable. Now you call us to extend a welcome to others. Help us make space in our homes and hearts and at our tables for those who need our welcome and love. In your name we pray. Amen.

I Want to WALK as a CHILD of the LIGHT

I want to walk as a child of the light.
I want to follow Jesus.
God set the stars to give light to the world.
The star of my life is Jesus.

I want to see the brightness of God.
I want to look at Jesus.
Clear Sun of Righteousness, shine on my path,
and show me the way to the Father.

Refrain:
In him there is no darkness at all.
The night and the day are both alike.
The Lamb is the light of the city of God.
Shine in my heart, Lord Jesus.

Words and Music: Kathleen Thomerson, 1966

SUNDAY
Song-Prayer

Start out by listening to, singing, or reading meditatively the first stanza of "I Want to Walk as a Child of the Light." Spend some moments in silence and let the words and the music enter your mind and heart. What word or phrase invites attention?

Read through or listen to the stanza again. This time, listen to what the hymn is saying to you today. Is there a message you are hearing for the first time? What is God saying through this tune or these words?

Pray the song-prayer below. Sing or read the lines to the song, followed by the prayer. (If listening to a recording of the song, play the section indicated and then pause.) Spend a moment in silence, and then continue to the next phrase.

If you feel led, write a song-prayer and record it in your journal. Close this meditation time by singing or reading the hymn again.

I want to walk as a child of the light.
I want to follow Jesus.

God of light and life, I hunger for you. My whole self longs for you. I want to follow you, to do as you will, to be your hands and heart to the world around me.

(Silence)

God set the stars to give light to the world.
The star of my life is Jesus.

God, your stars shine brightly above me, like the Star of Bethlehem. May your brilliant star, Jesus, be my star too. May it guide me toward you in this Advent season.

(Silence)

In him there is no darkness at all.
The night and the day are both alike.

O loving God, you are my constant companion. In you there is no darkness, for "darkness is as light to you" (Ps. 139:12). Walk with me through my times of darkness. Help me remember that you are present in both my joy and my despair.

(Silence)

The Lamb is the light of the city of God.
Shine in my heart, Lord Jesus.

Brilliant God, you created Jesus to be your light to the world. May Christ's light shine through the clutter of this season, touching all people, touching me. Let the light of Christ shine into the depths and corners of my heart. Amen.

(Silence)

MONDAY

Seasons of Darkness and Light

I want to walk as a child of the light.
I want to follow Jesus.

This Advent hymn holds great meaning for me, living as I do in North America. In the midst of days when the sun is distant and the days are shortening, I sing an affirmation, "I want to walk as a child of the light." The promised coming of this child of the light mirrors the promise that, shortly after December 21, the days will begin again to lengthen. Christmas falls so close to the Northern Hemisphere's winter solstice that I think of Christ's coming as synonymous with the return of the sun.

I am very sensitive to the seasons of the earth. It's hard for me to imagine a Christmas in the summer or in the tropics. Northern Hemispheric bias has influenced everything about Advent and Christmas—from Advent candles to Christmas songs and carols such as "I'm Dreaming of a White Christmas" and "In the Bleak Midwinter."

But what about my neighbors in the south; how do they mark these days? They also want to walk as "children of the light." They have both day and night, and during the night, the stars shine just as brightly. They pray and sing and prepare their hearts for Christ's coming just like I do. They attempt, as I do, to find the meaning in the season, to repel the attempts by the culture to commercialize this sacred observance. They are generous in their forgiveness of my myopic North American biases, and they interpret the story in a way meaningful to them.

Perhaps Christians in the Southern Hemisphere celebrate the strength of the sun and the summer season as symbols of God's powerful presence in a tiny, helpless baby. Perhaps they rejoice in the abundance of the earth as a sign of God's generous gifts to humankind. Certainly they read the same scriptures and look with longing toward the birth of God in a stable, come to shine in our hearts and in our struggling world.

All of us Christians around the world carry the same desire: to walk as children of the light, to follow Jesus as he leads us in a ministry of hope and love to the whole creation.

REFLECTION

Imagine celebrating Advent and Christmas in a different part of the world. How would you experience Jesus' birth during the summer (or winter) season? How is the experience the same as that where you live? How is it different?

Make a list of this season's characteristics that are the same, no matter where people live.

Pray for people who live in a different part of the world.

PRAYER

God of Darkness and Light, shine on the world and shine on me. Help me remember that no matter where I live, you send your gift of love to all people. Whether I see snow or sand, evergreen or palm trees, your presence speaks to me of hope for the world. In gratitude I pray for all the world and its people. Amen.

TUESDAY
Hungering for God

God set the stars to give light to the world.
The star of my life is Jesus.

I'm afraid of the dark. There, I've said it: I'm afraid of the dark. Some people love the nighttime, its quiet and still-ness. But not me! When darkness comes, my anxiety rises a bit. When I'm troubled, the darkness makes me feel more so—more anxious, more afraid, more worried.

In the morning, I'm one of those people who jump out of bed and function as soon as the alarm goes off. I work best in the morning. It's also my favorite time of day—early morning when the sun is coming up and the birds are flocking around the feeder for their breakfast.

I love the morning light, how it warms the earth, bathing each tree, each plant, and each person with its gentle presence. The light of the morning shrinks my nighttime fears, doubts, and worries—those anxieties that were so big the night before.

Another thing about me—every fall, as the days begin to shorten, I start to get a little melancholy. I have to start using my "grow light"—a full-spectrum light that sits in front of me while I eat breakfast. I use my light box in the mornings from September through March to supplement the diminished hours of sunshine. So, not only do I fear the dark, my body was created in a way that craves more light during the darker months of the year.

Maybe that's one reason I'm attracted to this song. "I want to walk as a child of the light. I want to follow Jesus. God set the stars to give light to the world. The star of my life is Jesus." Just as the world was created to hunger for light, just as my body hungers for the light of the sun, my soul was created to hunger for God.

I believe the Creator crafted each one of us to have a "God-hunger" within, a longing for a Higher Power to be present in our lives. The God-hunger is an inner yearning to connect to something bigger than ourselves. The star of my life—that which warms me and comforts me, gives me nourishment, and helps me grow—is Jesus, my Higher Power, the Holy Spirit, God.

The psalmist said it this way: "As a deer longs for flowing streams, / so my soul longs for you, O God" (Ps. 42:1). "O God, . . . I seek you, / my soul thirsts for you; my flesh faints for you, / as in a dry and weary land where there is no water" (Ps. 63:1).

All humanity was created with a longing to be connected to God, to be children of the light. I want to walk as a child of the light, to drink deeply from God's living water, to allow God's light to illuminate all the shadows inside me.

REFLECTION

Write on a card or sticky note one of the psalm verses above (Ps. 42:1 or Ps. 63:1). Carry it throughout the day today. When you feel overwhelmed or distracted, take a few moments of quiet. (Shut the door, turn off the phone, close the e-mail program.)

Read the verse(s) several times while taking deep breaths. With each exhaling breath, allow inner clutter and distractions to leave. With each inhaling breath, breathe in

God's warmth and peace. Exhale clutter. Inhale peace. Breathe for five minutes. Before reentering life, pray a prayer of thanks to God for the gifts of light, breath, and peace.

PRAYER

"As a deer longs for flowing streams, / so my soul longs for you, O God" (Ps. 42:1). Open my body, mind, and spirit that I may receive your gifts of light and breath and peace. Amen.

WEDNESDAY
The Empty Place Within

I want to walk as a child of the light.
I want to follow Jesus.

God created inside each of us an empty place—a place that can be filled only by God. This empty place, the source of God-hunger, challenges us, especially when we feel stressed by life.

I try to satisfy my God-hunger with things other than God. When I'm not tuned in to my true self or connected with God, I attempt to fill up that empty space with substitutes—TV, food, shopping.

For some, filling the empty place with substances other than God becomes an addiction. The empty place longs—demands—to be filled, so we experiment with all sorts of things—alcohol, work, caffeine. But only a connection with God will truly feed that interior hunger.

The Advent season overflows with false hungers. Lives are out of control with busyness and deadlines. We face pressure to finish tasks at work or school before the holidays begin. Calendars are full at home and church, full of parties, extra choir rehearsals, Christmas programs at church and school. Every day, the shopping countdown warns us that there are only fifteen (fourteen, thirteen . . .) shopping days left until Christmas. And don't forget that we're also supposed to get our spiritual life ready for the coming of the Christ child!?

We hunger for control, for something that will alleviate this craziness we feel. We yearn for something that will fill the gnawing emptiness below the busyness. We try to fix it by working longer, drinking more caffeine, doing more or by numbing the discomfort with food, TV, or alcohol.

When we find ourselves in a quiet place or alone, sometimes all we can hear is the chorus of inner voices reminding us of the things we need to do. It seems so radical, so outrageous, so impossible to take time to stop or pray or connect with God. But by taking that time, we become aware of the empty place inside. In this way, God can reach us to nourish our God-hunger. God pours love, peace, and comfort into the emptiness. When we take time to stop and become aware of the God-hunger, we can allow God to fill us with a renewing, nourishing spirit.

Prayer and meditation in the midst of chaos offer a radical antidote for the cultural insanity that many of us experience. God created in us an empty place. God can fill that empty place if we allow it.

REFLECTION

How do you feel the God-hunger within? Is it a particular physical sensation or an emotion? Do you recognize it, or is it disguised? How do you fill it?

What obstacles keep you from taking time with God? What would be one action you could take today to overcome one of these challenges?

When you become aware that you are trying to satisfy a God-hunger with food, TV, alcohol, or shopping, for example, try these steps: (1) Stop what you are doing. (2) Concentrate on the hunger inside and the desire to fill it with something other than God. (3) Pray the prayer below to turn this hunger over to God and ask God to fill the empty place.

PRAYER

God of Life, whatever I am looking for in [fill in the blank] may I find in you. Thank you for making me aware of the inner hunger I have for you. Fill me and make me whole. Amen.

THURSDAY
Children of Action

I want to see the brightness of God.
I want to look at Jesus.

Our desire to be children of the light leads us to action—both individually and as a community. We walk as children of the light. We follow Jesus. We live the Jesus Story.

We not only have a God-hunger inside us, but we also have a desire to see God's brightness, God's goodness all around us. We can see God every day, even today. We can see Jesus all around us in the people we meet, the children we serve, our coworkers, and family members. How many times a day do we see Jesus? How many times a day do we see the brightness of God? And how many times do we miss seeing Jesus because we are too busy or too preoccupied, too worried or angry or tired? We become wrapped up in our own lives, and we are blinded by filters of assumption and prejudice.

A couple of years ago I was sitting at Starbucks having a meeting with a coworker. I was talking (I'm sure) about some incredible idea of mine when I noticed a tall, scruffy-looking older man shuffling toward me. His hair was a mess, and he walked with a cane. As he passed near me, I instinctively reached down to secure my purse. A few seconds later, my coworker leaned over to me and said, "Did you see that? Johnny Cash just went into the men's room."

Oh, my gosh! I thought Johnny Cash was a homeless person. If I can't recognize Johnny Cash, how am I going to notice Jesus in the people around me? I have to pay attention, to free myself from the fears, assumptions, and prejudices almost woven into my very cells. I have to challenge myself to let go of the baggage I carry around, to move beyond my comfort zone, to put myself in proximity with people who are different from me so that I have opportunity to grow out of those old assumptions and prejudices.

I want to see the brightness of God in the people I meet —that's the only way to see Jesus. I want to see God in not only the homeless, the children, the poor, the other, the stranger, but also in the coworker with whom I am annoyed, the church member who drives me nuts, the family member at whom I'm angry.

REFLECTION

When in the past few days have you seen Jesus? What are the filters—the prejudices and assumptions—that keep you from seeing the brightness of God?

PRAYER

God of Brightness, forgive me for the times when I am blinded from seeing you in those around me. Open the eyes of my heart that I might see you today in unexpected places. Amen.

FRIDAY
God Is Present

In him there is no darkness at all.
The night and the day are both alike.

This phrase reminds me that God permeates everything—the night that I fear and the morning that I welcome. God—and God's grace—surrounds us throughout all of life, the easy, loving parts and the hard, difficult, scary times. God lives in both the night and the day—they are just alike to God. When we face times of darkness in our personal lives, in our families, in our community or world, God moves close to us, loving us and holding our hands even if we are not aware of it. Even if we think God is absent.

A number of years ago, I went through a difficult personal time, a sort of dark night of the soul. I wasn't sure God really existed. And if God did exist, I was mad at God because I was hurting and didn't see how God could let that happen to me. You may have had a similar time in your life, when you were struggling and hurting and you couldn't feel God's love.

Throughout my struggle, I could not go to church. I was absent for a long time. During that time, though, other people became God's representatives to me. Other people loved me with grace-filled love. Other people believed in God on my behalf. Other people trusted for me when I had no trust and sat with me when I felt alone. Many of those people were members of my church family. They did not let go, and they did not let me struggle alone. They called and sent cards and letters. They prayed for me. They were representatives of the God of love, who sees the night and day, in whom there is no darkness at all.

When we are facing a dark night of the soul, when we are sick or grieving, when we have hurt others or have been hurt by them, we are not alone. The God of darkness and light stays beside us. And the God of darkness and light sends messengers—messengers like you and me—to remind us that we are not alone.

We are beloved children of God, deserving of comfort, healing, and joy. We worship a God in whom there is no darkness, who loves us no matter who we are or what we have done. And we are called to be children of the light, doers, messengers to others of God's love and grace, God's comfort and forgiveness.

REFLECTION

Advent is a lonely time of year to be struggling or facing difficulty. Think of someone who is having a hard time right now. Consider reaching out to this person through a visit, phone call, card, or e-mail. Send a message of love and grace, reminding this person that he or she is a special child of God.

PRAYER

Come, Holy Spirit. Come into our lives today and show us how to be children of the light for each other and for the world. Amen.

SATURDAY
Shine in My Heart

Shine in my heart, Lord Jesus.

This simple phrase represents both a deep-felt longing and an invitation to a way to live during Advent.

"Shine in my heart," the place where I experience God, the heart where I experience the God-hunger. I long for the light of Christ to shine in my heart, nurturing and sustaining my spirit.

"Shine in my heart"—illuminate the dark places in my heart: the sadness, grief, anger. Illuminate the dark places in my mind: the resentments, the frustrations. Illuminate the dark places of my spirit: the depression, the anxiety, the fear. Shine in my heart, Lord Jesus, and lighten the heaviness that paralyzes my action. Heal the wounds and sins that keep me separated from God.

"Shine in my heart"—show me the way through the confusing paths I may take, the choices too numerous, the infinite options of postmodern life. Shine in my heart as a beacon of guidance, leading me through the chaos of these days.

"Shine in my heart"—so that my life may mirror Christ's heart and mind and hands in the world. May my heart be filled with God's love so that I may be the heart and hands and words of Christ in the world. May God guide me to acts of love, compassion, and understanding in my thoughts, words, and deeds.

"Shine in my heart"—so that I may prepare my life for the coming of the Christ child.

REFLECTION

Think about the phrase "Shine in my heart, Lord Jesus." What thoughts, feelings, or memories does this phrase evoke in you? What places in your life, family, or community need the light of Christ today?

Pray for these people or situations. Ask that the light of Christ might shine deep into each place.

PRAYER

THE PRAYER OF SAINT FRANCIS

Lord, make me an instrument of thy peace;
where there is hatred, let me sow love;
where there is injury, pardon;
where there is doubt, faith;
where there is despair, hope;

where there is darkness, light;
and where there is sadness, joy.
O Divine Master,
grant that I may not so much seek
to be consoled as to console;
to be understood, as to understand;
to be loved, as to love;
for it is in giving that we receive;
it is in pardoning that we are pardoned;
and it is in dying that we are born to eternal life.

o COME, *o* COME, EMMANUEL

O come, O come, Emmanuel,
and ransom captive Israel,
that mourns in lonely exile here
until the Son of God appear.

Refrain:
Rejoice! Rejoice!
Emmanuel
shall come to thee, O Israel.

Words: 9th-century Latin
Music: 15th-century French

The words to this Advent hymn were translated from ninth-century Latin prayers of the Catholic Church. They were known as the "Great Antiphons" or "O Antiphons" (referring to the use of "O come" at the beginning of each antiphon). It is thought that a different antiphon was sung in the monastery on succeeding nights leading up to Christmas. Each antiphon bears a different name for the Messiah.

According to scholar Mother Thomas More, the tune, "Veni Emmanuel," was used as a processional for a community of fifteenth-century French Franciscan nuns living in Lisbon, Portugal. When I hear this hymn, I think of monks or nuns in candlelit cathedrals singing hope in the darkness of the nights before Christmas.

SUNDAY

Song-Prayer

Start by listening to, singing, or reading meditatively the first stanza of "O Come, O Come, Emmanuel." Spend some moments in silence, allowing the words and the music to enter your mind and heart. What word or phrase invites attention?

Read through or listen to the stanza again. This time, listen for what the hymn says to you today. Is there a message you are hearing for the first time? What is God saying through this tune or these words?

Pray the following song-prayer. Sing or read the first lines from the song, then the prayer. (If listening to a recording of the song, play the section indicated, then pause.) Spend a moment in silence and then continue to the next section.

If you feel led, write a song-prayer and record it in your journal. Close this meditation time by singing or reading the hymn again.

O come, O come, Emmanuel,
and ransom captive Israel,

Come, Emmanuel, God-with-Us. Come quickly to our hearts and our spirits. Save us from the captivity of busyness and preoccupation, consumerism and desire for more.

(Silence)

that mourns in lonely exile here
until the Son of God appear.

Come, Emmanuel, God-with-Us. Let us know your presence in the midst of our loneliness and grief, our sickness and sorrow. We thirst; we long for you even as we fill our lives with so many things. Open our eyes that we might see you in the faces around us, that we might hear your voice in the noises filling the air.

(Silence)

Rejoice! Rejoice!
Emmanuel shall come to thee, O Israel.

Emmanuel, God-with-Us, we await you with songs of joy and shouts of praise. Help us to make spaces in our busy lives in order to welcome your coming. Come, Creator. Come, Spirit. Come, Christ. Make your home in us today. Amen.

(Silence)

MONDAY

Prayer Movement

O come, O come, Emmanuel

This Advent hymn invites us into a particular prayer sequence. The structure of the hymn moves us naturally through a liturgical sequence that includes the elements of invitation, naming, petition, and praise.

INVITATION

Each stanza starts with the phrase "O come." During these days of anticipation, we invite the coming of the Messiah. *Come*, our hearts cry out in longing expectation. We've waited years for Christ to be present in our wounded world. Come soon, come quickly. Come.

NAMING

We name that for which we hope. "Come, Emmanuel." (*Emmanuel* means "God is with us." See Isa. 7:14 and Matt. 1:23.) When Emmanuel comes into our lives, we realize that God-with-Us has been here all along; we just hadn't noticed. We had to issue the invitation, to open the door to our heart, before we could feel God's presence with us. *God is with us*, we realize.

PETITION

After we have invited and received God, then we make our request. "Ransom captive Israel, that mourns in lonely exile here." "Bind all peoples in one heart and mind." So many requests crowd our hearts—some big, some small, some for the world, some for our families or for ourselves. God knows our requests even before we speak them in our hearts, but we make those requests known, placing them into God's hands by naming them.

PRAISE

The final movement of this hymn is praise. "Rejoice! Rejoice! Emmanuel shall come to thee, O Israel." Rejoice that God is with us. Rejoice that God sends Christ to this world. Rejoice that we are heard in our petitions. Rejoice that Emmanuel, God-with-Us, shall come to us and to the people and places needing God the most.

REFLECTION

Try using this prayer movement today.

Invitation: Welcome God into your heart, into your consciousness. Consciously identify barriers that might exist there and imagine those barriers being taken down. Open the doors and the windows to your spirit.

Naming: After you have issued the invitation, name what you hope for. What do you most need today? presence? ("Emmanuel: God is with us"); freedom from worry or conflict? ("Prince of Peace"); love? ("Loving God"); comfort? ("Gentle, Loving God"); wisdom? ("Wonderful Counselor").

Petition: Make your request. Don't be shy. God already knows your heart's desire before you speak it. Write down your petitions, speak them aloud, or hold them quietly in your heart. Envision putting the requests into God's presence (perhaps into God's hands or placed in God's light).

Praise: Rejoice; thank God for hearing your prayers. Sing the refrain of "O Come, O Come, Emmanuel," or sing another hymn of praise. Pray Psalm 150 or write a short psalm of praise.

Close the quiet time with silence, thanking God for God's presence today.

PRAYER

[*Begin with silence.*] God, thank you for being present with me in whatever way I need. Thank you for taking these desires, hopes, and concerns into your loving heart. You are my Comfort, my Rock, my Peace, my [*fill in the name*]. I pray all these things in the name of the Christ, Amen.

TUESDAY
Rejoice! Rejoice!

Rejoice! Rejoice!
Emmanuel shall come to thee, O Israel.

The third Sunday of Advent is historically called *Gaudete* Sunday, a name taken from the first word of the Latin Mass meaning "Rejoice." During this season of reflection and preparation, we take time out to rejoice in the promised coming of Emmanuel, God-with-Us.

We rejoice in the many gifts that God has given us. We proclaim with the psalmist: "The LORD has done great things for us, and we rejoiced" (Ps. 126:3). We give thanks for the abundant gifts of home and nourishment, family and friends, times of work and times of rest. We give thanks that we are beloved children of God.

We rejoice that Emmanuel, God-with-Us, stands with us in the midst of both our joys and our sorrows. "Rejoice in the Lord always; again I will say rejoice" (Phil. 4:4). We give thanks that God walks with us through all ages and stages of our life, that God loves us no matter our status or situation.

Even the earth and the heavens rejoice in God's greatness! "The wilderness and the dry land shall be glad, / the desert shall rejoice and blossom; / like the crocus it shall blossom abundantly, / and rejoice with joy and singing" (Isa. 35:1-2).

"Rejoice! Emmanuel shall come to thee . . ." This phrase promises that the gift will come, no matter what. We don't have to do anything. The gift comes to us where we are right now, not because of what we have done but because we are children of God. Rejoice and give thanks. Emmanuel shall come to you, to me, and to all the heavens and the earth.

REFLECTION

One way to "rejoice in the Lord always" is to make a "gratitude list" every day. Get a notebook in which to keep a gratitude list or keep your list in a journal. Each day during meditation time, write down everything for which you are grateful. Some days this exercise may be more difficult than others. But always write down at least ten items on the gratitude list.

Expand the gratitude list beyond a list of things. Use all five senses to help remember characteristics in the self or others that we cherish. (For example: my sense of compassion for others, the softness of a child's skin, the sound of my spouse's laugh.)

Carry this list with you and think of it during the day. Allow yourself to rejoice, to be happy for the gifts you have received from God.

PRAYER

Great Giver of Gifts, I rejoice in you today. During this Advent season of joy, may I rejoice in your greatness and your love for all the earth and its peoples. Help me to spread this great joy to all I might meet today. Amen.

WEDNESDAY
Ransom the Captives

O come, O come, Emmanuel,
and ransom captive Israel.

Marcus was a little boy in our church's after-school tutoring program. His little brother and sister also attended the program. I knew I was not supposed to have favorites when working with kids, but they were my favorites.

Marcus and his siblings were beautiful. One was a little skinny; another, a little chubby. But each had the same infectious smile and compelling energy. They welcomed me with smiles and hugs on the afternoons I arrived to staff the computer room. "It's my turn!" they called out before anyone else had seen me and claimed a place in line. Their intense desire to learn left me grinning all day.

I didn't know much about the children's family situation. I assumed, since they lived in the inner city and came to our tutoring program, that they lacked many benefits and privileges given to other kids.

But I was astounded to learn from a fellow worker that Marcus figured he would not live past his teenage years. Boys in the neighborhood witnessed so much crime, drug activity, and violence that Marcus predicted he would be shot or knifed and die before he turned eighteen. This hopelessness from a nine- or ten-year-old child! Lord, have mercy.

This story about Marcus deeply affected me. Living as many of us do—sheltered in a life of relative affluence and security—I don't hear, don't know the stories of today's Marcuses. But these are the "little ones" to whom our Savior came at Christmas.

Come, Emmanuel, and ransom Marcus from his fears and his captivity. "Rejoice, Rejoice," the angels sing. Emmanuel has come to Marcus, to his siblings, to children, young and old who need Christ's love. This Emmanuel says, "You are beloved children of God. Don't give up hope, for I am walking with you every moment. No matter what happens, I am with you and I love you."

Marcus's gift to me is this message from God: "Love the children. Share my love with others, especially the lost and the least of these. If you love me, feed my lambs" (see John 21).

Come, Emmanuel, and ransom the poor and the hopeless who live in the inner city, the barrios, and the slums of the world. Ransom those who are captives to poverty. Come, Emmanuel, and ransom those with money and power, affluence and blindness to need. Ransom those who are captive to sheltered lives of privilege.

Come, Emmanuel; come, Holy Spirit. Be with us all and set us free from captivity.

REFLECTION

From what captivities do you need to be ransomed today?

What one action can you take today to reach one of Christ's lost or least? Commit to carry out that action.

PRAYER

Ransom me, O God of freedom, from my captivity. Set me free from the things that keep me in bondage. Empower me to take action to reach one of your least or lost. May I see your face in all those I meet today, and may I be your hands and heart in this captive world. Amen.

THURSDAY
Those Who Mourn

That mourns in lonely exile here
until the Son of God appear.

This Advent hymn says God comes for everyone—the joyous *and the grieving*, those who celebrate *and those who mourn*. "Ransom captive Israel, that mourns in lonely exile here." Israel, captive in a foreign land, exiles stolen away from their home. Israel—the children of God—longing to be home, longing to be free; Israel longing for the coming of Emmanuel, God-with-Us.

This message about God's coming speaks to the one who has lost a family member. God comes to the woman who feels in exile in her own marriage, for the man who grieves the loss of life dreams. God comes to the child who lives on the street, for the parents who struggle to feed and clothe their children. God comes to the one whose loneliness or depression intensifies every Christmas. Emmanuel —God-with-Us—comes to comfort the grieving, the mourning, the sad, the lonely.

This promise awaits us and all those who mourn—and we rejoice. "Rejoice! Rejoice! Emmanuel shall come to thee, O Israel."

But this rejoicing, this gratitude to God, does not *take away* our feelings. This Advent hymn does not say to a hurting person, "Get over it. You've been sad long enough. Be happy and come to the party." It says that Emmanuel— God-with-Us—is coming to us, to meet us wherever we are—happy or sad, joyous or grieving. God comes to stand with us, whatever our condition. And we thank God for that promised gift of presence.

Rejoice! Emmanuel comes to the sad and the lonely person. God stands with us, no matter what we are feeling or experiencing. Rejoice! God does not mind that we are grieving or mourning. In fact, God comes especially for the least and the lost. Thanks be to God.

REFLECTION

Consider the places of sadness or grief during this Advent season. Pray for God's healing presence.

What hurts do you carry during this time of year? What trusted friend or pastor might listen to your story? In what ways can you express your gratitude to God, even in the midst of sadness and pain?

PRAYER

God of Love, many are lonely and grieving during this Advent season. Send your healing Spirit to all who mourn, that they may know your comforting presence with them. Amen.

FRIDAY
God of Many Names

O come, O come, Emmanuel, . . .
O come, thou Wisdom from on high, . . .
O come, O come, great Lord of might, . . .
O come, thou Root of Jesse's tree, . . .
O come, thou Key of David, . . .
O come, thou Dayspring, . . .
O come, Desire of nations, . . .

Many of us have grown up with a rather limited list of names for the Almighty—God, Lord, Father, King, Jesus, Spirit. But scripture and tradition paint a much broader portrait than we can imagine. Some people feel threatened by the thought of various names for the Divine. I believe, however, that increasing my "God vocabulary" actually enhances my relationship with the One who created me.

From this Advent hymn emerge a number of different names for the Almighty. Some of these names evoke the Promised Coming as foretold in the scriptures: "Key of David" (see Isa. 22:22) and "Root of Jesse's Tree." "Root of Jesse's Tree" is a reference to Isaiah 11:1: "A shoot shall come out from the stump of Jesse, and a branch shall grow out of his roots." Jesse was the grandson of Ruth and Boaz and the father of David. Jesus, the Christ child, came from the lineage of David and Jesse, as foretold by the prophet Isaiah.

Ruth was a Moabite, not a Jew; she married one of Naomi's sons. Ruth, faithful to Naomi after the death of Ruth's husband, journeyed back to Naomi's land and married Boaz, a relative of her mother-in-law's. Upon the birth of her grandson, the women proclaimed Naomi blessed. "[This child] shall be to you a restorer of life and a nourisher of your old age; for your daughter-in-law who loves you, who is more to you than seven sons, has borne him" (Ruth 4:15). Buried in the genealogy of the Christ lies this story of two brave women who were faithful to their God and to their friendship.

Other names in this hymn evoke various characteristics of God: "Emmanuel," "Wisdom," "great Lord of might," "Dayspring" (see Luke 1:78, KJV), "Desire of nations."

This Advent and Christmas season of the year offers the gift of additional names and images of God and Christ: "Bright Morning Star," "Holy Child," "Son of the Most High." Isaiah's names for the Messiah are repeated every Advent season through song:

> For a child has been born for us,
>> a son given to us;

authority rests upon his shoulders;
    and he is named
Wonderful Counselor, Mighty God,
    Everlasting Father, Prince of Peace (Isa. 9:6).

We are invited to consider what names for God or Christ spring forth from our heart, from our spiritual center. What names do we carry within that strengthen our relationship with the Creator of the universe?

REFLECTION

Make a list of the names for God or Christ that carry meaning for you. Which names don't make sense to you? Are there names to which you cannot relate? What new names might you add to your God vocabulary? Consider this question: "What does God call me?" Carry these questions with you throughout your day.

PRAYER

God of many names, you indeed are greater than I can ever imagine. As you reveal to me your infinite nature, may I never be far from you. Help me to listen to your voice guiding and loving me and to listen ever more closely for that name by which you call me. Amen.

SATURDAY
One Heart and Mind

*Bind all peoples
in one heart and mind.*

I recently had the opportunity to help staff a weeklong spiritual retreat for persons with HIV/AIDS. The retreat was at a nearby state park. We staff arrived twenty-four hours ahead to prepare for the participants. We didn't know much about the people who were coming. We knew their names and where they were from. We knew that some were homeless. All were living with HIV/AIDS.

The church buses pulled up, and fifteen people got off. I could sense nervousness among both the staff and the participants as we looked at one another for the first time. Then one staffer stood up, called out, "Welcome!" and offered a hug to the first participant he reached. Soon we too were welcoming, introducing ourselves, and hugging the newcomers.

Our group was quite diverse racially, economically, and in other ways. But we were brought together by the call from a loving God that all people deserve to be cared for, nurtured in body, mind, and spirit.

Long ago Jesus crossed cultural and religious lines to embrace those who were different, unclean, unseen. This special retreat gave me the privilege to serve as Jesus did, reaching out and embracing those who are the lepers or tax collectors of our culture. Like Jesus, we reached out, sometimes beyond our comfort zone, to today's outcasts—

the poor, the homeless, IV drug users, sexual minorities, those with HIV/AIDS.

By the end of the retreat, we—staff and participants — were bound in the heart and mind of a loving God. We were "no longer Jew or Greek, . . . slave or free, . . . male and female," white or black, HIV-positive or HIV-negative, rich or poor. We were all "one in Christ Jesus" (Gal. 3:28). As we closed our week together with a service of Holy Communion, we shared a common loaf and cup, reminded that we are all one in Christ Jesus.

REFLECTION

Jesus called his disciples to serve others. Service in Christ's loving spirit brings us into union with the heart, mind, and hands of Christ. Today, plan a time to engage in service to others. Here are a few suggestions:

- Inquire about participating in a feeding program or delivering holiday food baskets.

- Check for volunteer options at local homeless shelters.

- Contact a local HIV/AIDS support center and ask about the special needs during the holiday season.

PRAYER

Bind us, O God, in one heart and mind, that we may be one people serving you, loving you, proclaiming your hope to all the world. Amen.

Lo, How a ROSE
E'er BLOOMING

Lo, how a Rose e'er blooming
from tender stem hath sprung!
Of Jesse's lineage coming, as those of old have sung.
It came, a floweret bright, amid the cold of winter,
when half spent was the night.

Isaiah 'twas foretold it, the Rose I have in mind;
with Mary we behold it, the Virgin Mother kind.
To show God's love aright, she bore to us a Savior,
when half spent was the night.

Words: 15th-century German; trans. by Theodore Baker, 1894
Music: Alte Catholische Geistliche Kirchengesäng, 1599

"Lo, How a Rose E'er Blooming" is a fifteenth-century German carol based on Isaiah 11:1: "A shoot shall come out from the stump of Jesse, and a branch shall grow out of his roots."

According to some scholars, "the rose" originally referred to Mary, the mother of Jesus. Medieval symbols often portrayed the "tree of Jesse" as a rose plant. Mary was the shoot that came from the stump of Jesse (Jesus' ancestor, the father of David), and Jesus was the bloom that came upon that branch.

This hymn with its haunting melody evokes an ancient time, the mystery of roses blooming in the winter, of light that overcomes darkness, of ancient prophecies fulfilled.

SUNDAY

Song-Prayer

Start by listening to, singing, or reading meditatively the first stanza of "Lo, How a Rose E'er Blooming." Spend some moments in silence and let the words and the music enter your mind and heart. What word or phrase invites attention?

Read through or listen to the stanza again. This time, listen to what the hymn is saying today. Is there a message you are hearing for the first time? What is God saying through this tune or these words?

Pray the following song-prayer. Sing or read the lines to the song, followed by the prayer. (If listening to a recording of the song, play the section indicated and then pause.) Spend a moment in silence, and then continue to the next phrase.

If you feel led, write a song-prayer and record it in your journal. Close this meditation time by singing or reading the hymn again.

Lo, how a Rose e're blooming
from tender stem hath sprung!

God of all creation, you have given us the most beautiful gift of all—your love in the form of a tiny baby. We await with joy the birth of this fragile, elegant gift.

(Silence)

Of Jesse's lineage coming,
as those of old have sung.

God of all creation, we have waited long years for your incarnation. Our stories and our memories are filled with songs of hope and praise for the one who is to come.

(Silence)

It came, a floweret bright,
amid the cold of winter,

God of all creation, you create miracles that astound us. Through your grace, flowers bloom in winter, and love shines through barriers of hatred.

(Silence)

when half spent
was the night.

God of all creation, even in the middle of the darkest night you are present with your sustaining love and grace.

Creating God, we await your miraculous, vulnerable birth in a manger. Amen.

(Silence)

―――――◆◆◆◆◆―――――

MONDAY
Mary Listened

―――――◆◆◆◆◆―――――

Isaiah 'twas foretold it, the Rose I have in mind;
with Mary we behold it, the Virgin Mother kind.
To show God's love aright, she bore to us a Savior,
when half spent was the night.

It's really a remarkable story—that an angel of the Lord appeared in ancient times to a young, unmarried woman and told her that she would bear a child who "will be called the Son of the Most High" (Luke 1:32). Perhaps even more remarkable is her response, "Here am I, the servant of the LORD; let it be with me according to your word" (Luke 1:38). Mary's story teaches us important spiritual lessons.

Mary listened. The angel said to her, "Greetings, favored one! The Lord is with you" (Luke 1:28). The scriptures say that Mary was "much perplexed by his words and pondered what sort of greeting this might be" (Luke 1:29). That may have put it mildly! But still Mary listened.

As she continued to listen, she heard the angel say, "You will conceive in your womb and bear a son" (Luke 1:31). An unsettling message for a young unmarried woman to hear:

she would become pregnant, and the child would be God's son. Amazing and astounding words—all heard by Mary. Mary listened to the call of God through the words of the angel. Mary, an ordinary woman from long ago, engaged in the spiritual discipline of listening.

God had a lot to say in the various stories surrounding Jesus' birth, and many other individuals engaged in the practice of listening. Zechariah and Elizabeth listened to God telling them that Elizabeth would have a child in her old age—and that he should be named John (see Luke 1:5-25, 57-80). Mary listened to the angel's news of her impending pregnancy and the future promise of the son she would birth. Joseph listened to the proclamation of the angel that he should not be afraid to take Mary as his wife because the son she would bear was from the Holy Spirit (see Matt. 1:18-25). All this listening was critical to the outcome of the story. What if Joseph had not listened to the angel and had refused to take Mary as his wife?

God also calls us to listen. We may not receive visits from winged angels proclaiming that God has a message for us, but God still speaks to us. Our task as those who would hear is to do all in our power to listen to God's voice speaking to us.

Our task is to quiet our minds and our spirits, to slow down enough to hear what God might be saying to us. We could hear God in the words of a hymn, prayer, or scripture at church or in our devotional time. We could hear a message through a situation we encounter in our day. We might even hear through a touch, a smile, or a word from a friend or stranger. As faithful people we need to "tune in" to the ways that God may be speaking to us.

The story of Mary reminds us to listen, for even in the midst of unlikely situations God may be speaking very important words to us.

REFLECTION

God may be speaking to you today. Be receptive; take several breaks during the day to rest, breathe, and reflect. Think about encounters with other people. Hold these situations in God's light and ask God, *What am I to hear from these experiences? these encounters?*

At the end of the day, take time to remember the day. Where did you experience God today? What messages did you hear from God?

PRAYER

God, in this week of anticipation, I listen for you. Sharpen my listening so that I might hear your voice through my encounters and experiences. Amen.

TUESDAY
Mary Trusted

Isaiah 'twas foretold it, the Rose I have in mind;
with Mary we behold it, the Virgin Mother kind.
To show God's love aright, she bore to us a Savior,
when half spent was the night.

Mary trusted. Not only did she listen, but Mary also trusted that she was not having a crazy hallucination brought on by fatigue or too much wine. She trusted that the message brought to her by the angel Gabriel came from God.

I wonder, *What did it take for Mary to trust God?* I can make up all sorts of postmodern story lines: Mary must have been raised by a family who believed in God. She probably had the remarkable faith in God women of that age possessed. She had heard the stories of faith throughout her life—the prophecy from Isaiah that someday a Messiah would come to free the people. She knew that God sent angels to speak to people.

But the truth is that when an angel of the LORD appeared to Mary and brought God's message to her, Mary listened and Mary trusted.

We experience trust in many forms today. Just driving a car down the street involves trust that other people will obey the laws of the road and will not run their cars into ours. We rely on industries of trust regarding our bank accounts, our mutual funds, and our retirement accounts. We purchase liability insurance to provide for the rare cases when defective products, human mistakes, or accidents break trust.

But trust in God often proves more difficult. God's not tangible. We know God exists, but we cannot see or touch God. Trust in God involves a level of faith that we might not always be able to feel. Trusting becomes more challenging when things are not going well or when we receive unwelcome surprises. How could Mary have trusted God when she heard that she was soon going to become a pregnant unmarried woman?

The scriptures offer many examples of people who trusted God even when it did not make sense to trust. The psalmist lays out his case before God:

My eye wastes away from grief,
>   my soul and body also.
For my life is spent with sorrow,
>   and my years with sighing;
>   my strength fails because of my misery,
>   and my bones waste away. (Ps. 31:9-10)

And yet, the psalmist proclaims, "But I trust in you, O LORD; I say, 'You are my God.' My times are in your hand" (Ps. 31:14-15).

We're called through the miraculous story of Mary, Joseph, and Jesus to trust God. We often carry many worries and fears, sometimes heightened by the season—worries about money, about safety, about the future. We worry about the health of family and friends—or ourselves. But we are called to have faith in the One who loved us even before we were born.

We join with the psalmist in proclaiming,

>   I trust in you, O LORD;
>   I say, "You are my God."
>   My times are in your hand; . . .
>   Let your face shine upon your servant;
>   save me in your steadfast love. (Ps. 31:14-16)

REFLECTION

Make a list of any fears and concerns you feel today. Read through the list and ask God to take each worry, each concern, and fill you with trust. Use the prayer, "God, I give you [this worry]. Shine your light on [this worry] and fill me with trust in you."

If you find yourself worrying during the day, say the prayer again. Imagine God's light shining on the problem or fear. Envision being filled with God's light and trust.

PRAYER

I trust in you, O Lord.
You are my God.
My times are in your hand.
Let your face shine upon me;
Save me in your steadfast love.
Amen. (Adapted from Psalm 31:14-16)

WEDNESDAY
Mary Believed

Isaiah 'twas foretold it, the Rose I have in mind;
with Mary we behold it, the Virgin Mother kind.
To show God's love aright, she bore to us a Savior,
when half spent was the night.

Mary believed. The message she heard was unbelievable, even bizarre, but Mary believed. She believed even through her doubts. Despite the consequences of her unusual situation, Mary believed. God calls us, like Mary, to believe, no matter what situation we face, to believe in God's presence and God's plan.

Believe—"to accept as true." "I believe . . ."—an action of faith for Christians since the days of Jesus' ministry. We believe in God. And we act on that belief in our lives as people of faith. What we believe shapes our actions.

Joseph believed the angel who told him, "Do not be afraid to take Mary as your wife, for the child conceived in her is from the Holy Spirit. She will bear a son, and you are to name him Jesus, for he will save his people from their sins" (Matt. 1:20-21). Joseph believed and "did as the angel of the Lord commanded him" (Matt. 1:24).

My friend Don believes in a God of justice who calls all people to witness to God's love and God's ministry to the poor and the outcasts. Don is a seventy-three-year-old minister and retired professor. He served six months in federal prison for protesting against a government-sponsored training institute that over the years has instructed military troops from Central and South America. Graduates of this school have committed brutal crimes, including the murders of four U.S. Catholic women and the murder of Archbishop Oscar Romero in El Salvador in 1980.

In Don's statement to the judge at his trial for civil disobedience, he said, "We must always seek to obey God rather than humans. My faith has also led me to be attentive to what I call a war against the poor. The shaping of policies that enrich the few and dishonor the poor, especially children, has become the tragedy of our time. . . . I stand before you, a seventy-three-year-old man who is guilty [of these charges] but proud to be able to make this witness."

Don's belief in God called him to walk peacefully onto the grounds of a military training institute, even though such trespassing resulted in a prison sentence. Mary's belief in God led her to follow the improbable path outlined by the angel Gabriel. Her hymn of praise expresses her belief in the God of justice who has

brought down the powerful from their thrones,
    and lifted up the lowly;
[who] has filled the hungry with good things,
    and sent the rich away empty. (Luke 1:52-53)

Thanks be to God for those who believe.

REFLECTION

What are your core beliefs? How well do your actions and priorities in life reflect your core beliefs?

PRAYER

Jesus said, "Do not fear. Only believe" (see Luke 8:40-56). Take me in your loving arms, O God, and let me feel your powerful Spirit. Take away my fears and my doubts that I may believe and act according to your desire for my life. May I learn more and more how to have my actions reflect my beliefs. In your name I pray. Amen.

THURSDAY
Mary Waited

Isaiah 'twas foretold it, the Rose I have in mind;
with Mary we behold it, the Virgin Mother kind.
To show God's love aright, she bore to us a Savior,
when half spent was the night.

Mary waited . . . for the birth of the Holy Child. She waited for God's promise to come true. And we, like Mary, wait during this season of Advent. We wait in anticipation, in active preparation, as Mary must have waited in preparation to bring a child into the world.

The anticipated coming of a child evokes images of grandmothers, aunts, and brothers crocheting special blankets, parents preparing a room with a crib and changing table, the rituals of baby showers and considering names for the one who is coming. Pregnancy is a time of waiting, but it's active waiting.

We wait actively in Advent also. We prepare for the rituals of Christmas celebrations. We prepare our homes, churches, schools, and offices with decorations. We plan meals and bake special foods. We think about friends and family with whom we communicate through Advent, Christmas, or Epiphany greetings.

And our hearts—our spirits—wait for the coming of the Christ child. We have worked hard during this Advent season to listen to God's voice, to turn over our fears and worries, to make a place in all the chaos to be able to welcome God into our lives and hearts.

During these last days of Advent, we continue to wait. May these final days include times of quiet. Open wide the door to our hearts. Let there be spaces, silences, and open places. Let us give ourselves the gift of time. "I wait for the LORD, my soul waits, and in [God's] word I hope" (Ps. 130:5). Wait for the Christ child in quiet and peace and hope.

REFLECTION

Give yourself the gift of time during these final days of Advent. Sit by a candle in silence. Take some moments for stillness after the household has gone to bed or before others get up in the morning. Turn off the TV and the telephone and make space just for God. Let go of unnecessary tasks; they can wait until after Christmas.

PRAYER

O Holy Child of Bethlehem, I wait for your coming. May my mind and spirit, my heart and life be ready for you. Come, Christ Jesus, and dwell in me. Amen.

FRIDAY
Mary Praised

Isaiah 'twas foretold it, the Rose I have in mind;
with Mary we behold it, the Virgin Mother kind.
To show God's love aright, she bore to us a Savior,
when half spent was the night.

Mary listened, trusted, believed, and waited. And finally, Mary praised God. Mary's hymn of praise, the Magnificat, presents a model for our time of rejoicing:

> My soul magnifies the Lord,
>   and my spirit rejoices in God my Savior,
>   for he has looked with favor on the lowliness of
>   his servant.
>   Surely, from now on all generations will call me
>   blessed;
>   for the Mighty One has done great things for me,
>   and holy is [God's] name. (Luke 1:46-49)

Mary praises God, remembering God's might acts. "God has lifted up the lowly; / [God] has filled the hungry with good things, / and sent the rich away empty" (Luke 1:52-53). Mary reminds us to praise God, to rejoice in the Lord. No matter what our circumstances, the Mighty One has done great things for us. We are blessed by the hand of the God who created us, the one who loves us no matter who we are or what we have done. Mary reminds us that God can take any of us, no matter how small or insignificant, and use us in God's holy work.

We are reminded during this holiday season to give gifts with joy and thanksgiving, remembering that, in giving, we commemorate God's great gift in the birth of God's Son. We are reminded to praise God for God's awesome love that we share with family, friends, and strangers. We are reminded that our lives, our love, our joy, and our blessings are gifts from the great God of love.

Blessed are we, for God has visited us in the form of a friend, a family member, a child, a stranger, and has proclaimed that we are chosen, loved children of God.

REFLECTION

Pray aloud Mary's hymn of praise, the Magnificat, in Luke 1:46-55.

What great things has God done for you? Make a list of God's mighty acts in your life.

Go through the day with a spirit of gratitude and praise. Watch for God's gifts today and thank God with the phrase, "My soul magnifies the Lord, and my spirit rejoices in God my Savior" (Luke 1:47).

PRAYER

God, great giver of love, may I, with Mary, listen, believe, wait on you, and praise you. For you are the source of all that is. Amen.

What CHILD Is THIS?

What child is this who, laid to rest,
on Mary's lap is sleeping?
Whom angels greet with anthems sweet,
while shepherds watch are keeping?

Refrain:
This, this is Christ the King,
whom shepherds guard and angels sing;
Haste, haste to bring him laud,
the babe, the son of Mary.

Words: William Chatterton Dix, 1865
(Luke 2:6-20; Matt. 2:1-12)
Music: 16th-century English melody

"What Child Is This?" was a poem written in 1865 by
William Chatterton Dix. Born in Bristol, England, in 1837,

Dix was manager of an insurance company in Glasgow. Over the course of his life, he wrote over forty hymns, including "As with Gladness, Men of Old."

Based on Luke 2:6-20 and Matthew 2:1-12, "What Child Is This?" paints a picture of the birth of the Christ child. Set to the sixteenth-century tune "Greensleeves," its close harmonies and gently lilting character evoke a quiet awe as the singer recounts the miracle of the holy birth.

CHRISTMAS EVE

What child is this who, laid to rest,
on Mary's lap is sleeping?
Whom angels greet with anthems sweet,
while shepherds watch are keeping?

Refrain:
This, this is Christ the King,
whom shepherds guard and angels sing;
Haste, haste to bring him laud,
the babe, the son of Mary.

It's Christmas Eve, a day of breathless anticipation. The child we have been awaiting will soon arrive! It's also a day of transition; we end our Advent period of waiting and preparation and begin our celebration of Christmas. (*Christmas*, from Old English words, means "Christ's festival.")

Mary and Joseph were also in transition on the eve of Jesus' birth. At the end of a long journey to Bethlehem, they stopped and waited. No more could be done. They waited with breathless anticipation, and perhaps a bit of fear, for the birth of this very special child.

Christmas Eve is often a comma, a pause, a stopping place. Our preparations complete, we have time to breathe, to rest, to savor the exquisite anticipation of this day. Our physical, mental, and spiritual preparations of the past weeks have been focused on this day, and now it has arrived. Cutting through the sounds of shopping malls still calling us to come and buy, we can hear the silence of a blessed night and a baby's first cry. This silence calls to our listening heart, and we reach out for it with gratitude and peace.

Among my favorite memories of Christmas Eve are candlelit services at my father's church. The glow of the candlelight softened the features of the sanctuary, illuminating the faces of family and friends. Having come home for the holidays, my brothers and I sang "What Child Is This?" as a part of the Christmas Eve worship service. When I sing the song now, I hear the sounds of our guitars and our voices blending together in harmony, the silence broken only by the music. What a blessing to be able to sing together, offering the gift of this hymn on the eve of Christ's birth.

Through these words we see the nativity, the newborn baby cradled in Mary's arms. Mary and Joseph look with amazement at this miracle, a precious, tiny boy given to them (and to the whole world but at least for now, to them). The stillness of the night is broken by sounds of angels singing, animals stirring, shepherds arriving to see this thing of which the angel had spoken.

On this day when Advent preparation flows into Christmas celebration, we allow ourselves room to savor the quiet, breathless anticipation to which we are called on this night. We wait with eager attention for the birth of a Savior.

REFLECTION

Let your focus today be one of waiting with breathless anticipation. How do you hear God's stillness calling to you through the continuing cultural clamor? Make time today for a connection with God. Plan to participate in worship at church or observe a Christmas Eve service with family at home.

Plan a candlelight Christmas Eve dinner with family. Prepare the table with a good tablecloth and the best dishes and silverware. Make this meal a special time of waiting.

PRAYER

Birthing God,
tonight we wait
with breathless anticipation
the coming
of the Christ child.
Quiet our hearts and minds
that we may receive you
in holy hospitality.
Amen.

CHRISTMAS DAY

Why lies he in such mean estate
where ox and ass are feeding?
Good Christians, fear, for sinners here
the silent Word is pleading.

Refrain:
This, this is Christ the King,
whom shepherds guard and angels sing;
haste, haste to bring him laud,
the babe, the son of Mary.

"Do not be afraid," the angel says, "I am bringing you good news of great joy for all the people: to you is born this day in the city of David a Savior, who is the Messiah, the Lord" (Luke 2:10-11).

Good news! Celebrate with songs in your hearts. The Messiah has come to all the people: to the young and the old, to the rich and the poor, to all peoples and all nations. Celebrate with feasting and praising. The Savior has come to bring peace on earth and comfort to all people. Celebrate the good news of great joy.

Today a Savior has come to *us*. The Holy Child comes not just to the world, but also to people like us, meeting us right where we are. Christ comes to us in our joy and happiness and in our sorrow or loneliness. No matter who we are or what we have done. No matter whether this is the best Christmas ever or one of the worst, "*to you* is born this day . . . a Savior, who is the Messiah, the Lord" (emphasis added).

"Glory to God in the highest heaven, and on earth peace among those whom [God] favors!" (Luke 2:14).

REFLECTION

In all that you do today, give thanks for the gift of Jesus. Pray for people, communities, or nations that are in conflict today. May God bring them peace.

PRAYER

Gentle, loving God,
you come to me this day
in the form of a tiny, vulnerable baby.
I look on you with wonder and gratitude.
Glory to you in the highest heaven,
and on earth, peace among all peoples and nations.
for it is in the name of your child, Jesus,
that we pray.
Amen.

AWAY in a MANGER
and other CHRISTMAS Favorites

Do not put Christmas away too soon—
keep the joy and the song going
for the whole season.
—Mary Anna Vidakovich
Sing to the Lord: Devotions for Advent*

INTRODUCTION TO THE TWELVE DAYS OF CHRISTMAS

December 25 is only the first day of Christmas. The Christmas celebration continues for twelve days, after which we celebrate the arrival of the kings who followed the star to find the holy babe. The awaited event is here! Don't put away the celebration just yet, but instead follow the Christmas journey all the way to Epiphany.

Every Christmas a good friend of mine gives me a huge Christmas shopping bag filled with twelve smaller bags.

* Nashville, Tenn.: The Upper Room, 1994, 83-84.

Inside each small sack I find a gift for me or for someone in my family (even the dog sometimes gets a gift). I'm grateful for this tradition of opening one gift each day of the twelve days of Christmas. This practice reminds me to keep celebrating Christ's nativity all the way to Epiphany.

In this final section, we continue our daily reflections. Listen to what God has to say to us now that we have completed our preparations and begun the great Christmas celebration.

DECEMBER 26
Second Day of Christmas

AWAY IN A MANGER

Away in a manger, no crib for a bed,
the little Lord Jesus laid down his sweet head.
The stars in the sky looked down where he lay,
the little Lord Jesus, asleep on the hay.

Words: Anonymous
Music: James R. Murray, 1887

SCRIPTURE

[Mary] gave birth to her firstborn son and wrapped him in bands of cloth, and laid him in a manger, because there was no place for them in the inn. (Luke 2:7)

REFLECTION

Jesus was born in a manger, a feeding trough for livestock.

What a surprising place for the birth of a Savior. Today,
look in unexpected places for God's presence.

PRAYER

God of surprises,
as we walk through the day,
keep our eyes open
and our senses tuned
to your presence
in unexpected places.
Amen.

DECEMBER 27
Third Day of Christmas

JOY TO THE WORLD

Joy to the world, the Lord is come!
Let earth receive her King;
let every heart prepare him room,
and heaven and nature sing,
and heaven and nature sing,
and heaven, and heaven, and nature sing.

Words: Isaac Watts, 1719
Music: Arranged from G. F. Handel by Lowell Mason, 1848

SCRIPTURE

Make a joyful noise to the LORD, all the earth;
break forth into joyous song and sing praises.

Sing praises to the LORD with the lyre,
    with the lyre and the sound of melody.
With trumpets and the sound of the horn
make a joyful noise before the King, the LORD. (Psalm
98:4-6)

REFLECTION

"Joy to the World" and Psalm 98 both refer to the earth singing God's praises. How do you see nature rejoicing today?

Write a psalm of rejoicing. Include the many ways you "sing praises" in your life, in your family, or in your church community.

PRAYER

Joyful Creator, I join with the earth and heavens in singing your praises. As the sun, the moon, and the stars shine above, may I shine with the brightness of your love. May I sing your praises as I hear the movement of the trees in the wind or the sounds of birds. May I rejoice with my body as I walk gently on your beautiful earth. Thank you God, for sending your Son, Jesus. Let all creation sing your praises. Amen.

DECEMBER 28
Fourth Day of Christmas

SILENT NIGHT, HOLY NIGHT
Silent night, holy night, all is calm, all is bright
round yon virgin mother and child.

Holy infant, so tender and mild, sleep in heavenly peace,
sleep in heavenly peace.

Words: Joseph Mohr, 1818; trans. by John F. Young
Music: Franz Gruber, 1818

SCRIPTURE

Mary treasured all these words and pondered them in
her heart. (Luke 2:19)

REFLECTION

Think back over the Advent and Christmas season thus far.
What interactions, situations, or events do you recall?
Look in detail at these "mental snapshots" and pick one or
two of them to treasure as special or meaningful. Write a
description of this memory in a journal. Consider writing
a prayer or poem to describe how you will treasure these
things, pondering them in your heart.

PRAYER

Holy infant,
we treasure you
and the gift of love
that you bring to us today.
Amen.

DECEMBER 29
Fifth Day of Christmas

THE FIRST NOEL

The first Noel the angel did say
was to certain poor shepherds in fields as they lay;
in fields where they lay keeping their sheep,
on a cold winter's night that was so deep.
Noel, Noel, Noel, Noel, born is the King of Israel.

Words and music: Traditional English carol

SCRIPTURE

In that region there were shepherds living in the fields,
keeping watch over their flock by night. (Luke 2:8)

REFLECTION

Who are the "poor shepherds" of today? Think about the
people you would not expect to be visited by angels and
given a special invitation to see the Christ child. Today,
watch for God's actions performed by those people.

PRAYER

Noel! Noel!
God's nativity is here!
Go, and see,
You poor and rich,

Peasant and King,
See the place
Where our Savior was born.
Amen.

DECEMBER 30
Sixth Day of Christmas

ANGELS WE HAVE HEARD ON HIGH

Angels we have heard on high
sweetly singing o'er the plains,
and the mountains in reply echoing their joyous strains.
Gloria, in excelsis Deo! Gloria, in excelsis Deo!

Words: Traditional French carol; trans. Crown of Jesus, 1862
Music: French carol melody, arr. by Edward Shippen Barnes

SCRIPTURE

Then an angel of the Lord stood before them, and the
glory of the Lord shone around them, and they were terrified. But the angel said to them, "Do not be afraid; for
see—I am bringing you good news of great joy for all the
people: to you is born this day in the city of David a
Savior, who is the Messiah, the Lord." (Luke 2:9-11)

REFLECTION

How can you share the "good news of great joy for all the
people" today? Write a letter, make a phone call, or send
an e-mail to someone who needs some good news.

PRAYER

"Gloria, in excelsis Deo!
Glory to God in the highest heaven!"
We hear the angels sing
their hymns of great joy.
For to us is born
a Savior, who is Christ the Lord.
Amen.

NEW YEAR'S EVE—DECEMBER 31
Seventh Day of Christmas

IT CAME UPON THE MIDNIGHT CLEAR

It came upon the midnight clear,
that glorious song of old,
from angels bending near the earth,
to touch their harps of gold:
"Peace on the earth, good will to all,
from heaven's all gracious King."
The world in solemn stillness lay,
to hear the angels sing.

Words: Edmund H. Sears, 1849
Music: Richard Storrs Willis, 1850

SCRIPTURE

Suddenly there was with the angel a multitude of the
heavenly host, praising God and saying,

"Glory to God in the highest heaven,
and on earth peace among those whom [God] favors!"
(Luke 2:13-14)

REFLECTION

Today the world celebrates the end of a calendar year.
Remember the many places around the earth where war or
strife reigns. Be in prayer especially for places and people
in need of God's peace.

PRAYER

God of the heavens and the earth,
We need your peace.
Send your gentle, fierce Spirit
To all the war-torn lands
And broken relationships.
Come, God of peace.
We need you today.
Amen.

JANUARY 1
Eighth Day of Christmas

BREAK FORTH, O BEAUTEOUS HEAVENLY LIGHT

Break forth, O beauteous heavenly light,
and usher in the morning;
O shepherds, shrink not with affright,
but hear the angel's warning.

This child, now weak in infancy,
our confidence and joy shall be,
the power of Satan breaking, our peace eternal making.

Words: Johann Rist, 1641; trans. John Troutbeck, ca. 1885
Music: Johann Schop, 1641; harmony by J. S. Bach, 1737

SCRIPTURE

For everything there is a season, and a time for every matter under heaven:
> a time to be born, and a time to die;
> a time to plant, and a time to pluck up what is planted;
> a time to kill, and a time to heal;
> a time to break down, and a time to build up;
> a time to weep, and a time to laugh;
> a time to mourn, and a time to dance;
> a time to throw away stones, and a time to gather stones together;
> a time to embrace, and a time to refrain from embracing;
> a time to seek, and a time to lose;
> a time to keep, and a time to throw away;
> a time to tear, and a time to sew;
> a time to keep silence, and a time to speak;
> a time to love, and a time to hate;
> a time for war, and a time for peace. (Eccl. 3:1-8)

REFLECTION

Think back over the past year. What "seasons" have you been through in the past twelve months?

Read the scripture slowly and think about how these seasons have played out in your life. Use this list of "seasons" to reflect on the past year.

Note any situations that might need healing or further closure. Ask God for help in healing any wounds you have experienced or have visited on others.

Close with a time of prayer, thanking God for the past year and asking for God's presence in any unresolved situations.

PRAYER

Loving God,
thank you for your presence
in the tiny details of our lives.
May you be with us in every season,
every situation
in the coming year.
Amen.

JANUARY 2
Ninth Day of Christmas

O COME, ALL YE FAITHFUL

O come, all ye faithful, joyful and triumphant,
O come ye, O come ye, to Bethlehem.
Come and behold him, born the King of angels;

Refrain:
O come, let us adore him, O come, let us adore him,
O come, let us adore him, Christ the Lord.

Words and music: John F. Wade, ca. 1743;
trans. Frederick Oakeley, 1841, and others

SCRIPTURE

The Word became flesh and lived among us, and we have seen his glory, the glory as of a father's only son, full of grace and truth. (John 1:14)

REFLECTION

What actions will you take today that mark you as one of the "faithful"? How will you adore Christ in your daily journey? Make a commitment to one faithful action today.

PRAYER

Holy Savior,
we come, joyfully,
to witness your birth.
Come, let us adore you,
Christ, the Lord.
Amen.

JANUARY 3
Tenth Day of Christmas

LOVE CAME DOWN AT CHRISTMAS

Love came down at Christmas,
Love all lovely, Love divine;
Love was born at Christmas;
star and angels gave the sign.

Words: Christina G. Rossetti, 1885
Music: Traditional Irish melody

SCRIPTURE

God's love was revealed among us in this way: God sent his only Son into the world so that we might live through him. (1 John 4:9)

REFLECTION

Read slowly through the words of the Christmas hymn "Love Came Down at Christmas." What word or phrase stands out, catches your attention?

Read through the words a second time and consider: *What feelings do the words evoke in me? What thoughts, images, or memories emerge?*

Read through the words a final time. How is God calling you through these words? What action, prayer, or revelation emerges through the message of this hymn?

PRAYER

God of angels, God of the star,
you are "Lovely, Love divine."
Fill our hearts with love now.
Let us be your sacred sign.
Amen.

JANUARY 4
Eleventh Day of Christmas

HE IS BORN

He is born, the holy Child,
play the oboe and bagpipes merrily!

He is born, the holy Child,
sing we all of the Savior mild.

Words: Traditional 19th-century French carol; trans. anonymous
Music: 18th-century French carol

Scripture

O sing to the LORD a new song,
for [the LORD] has done marvelous things. (Ps. 98:1)

Reflection

Consider what new "songs" you are singing during this Christmas season. How has your spiritual life changed as a result of observing Advent and Christmas?

Prayer

Holy Child of Bethlehem, praises herald your gentle birth. With grateful voice and lifted spirit, I sing new songs to you. For in you, God has brought joy and hope to all the earth. Amen.

January 5
Twelfth Day of Christmas

Go, Tell It on the Mountain

Go, tell it on the mountain,
over the hills and everywhere;
go, tell it on the mountain, that Jesus Christ is born.

While shepherds kept their watching
o'er silent flocks by night,
behold throughout the heavens there shown a holy light.

Words: John W. Work Jr., 1907
Music: African-American spiritual

SCRIPTURE

How beautiful upon the mountains
  are the feet of the messenger
    who announces peace,
  who brings good news,
    who announces salvation,
    who says to Zion, "Your God reigns." (Isa. 52:7)

REFLECTION

Today is the twelfth day of Christmas, the last day of the
Christmas celebration. Think back through this time of
Advent preparation and Christmas observance. Note the
exercises, prayers, or hymns that were especially meaningful.
Make a list of the practices, thoughts, and learnings to take
with you into the coming year. Give thanks that God has
been with you in a special way this Advent and Christmas.

PRAYER

Good news!
Announce it from the highest mountain.
Sing it from the lowest valley.
Call it from the tallest building
and whisper it from the poorest hut.
Good news, Good news!
Jesus Christ is born!
Amen.

January 6
Epiphany—Three Kings' Day

We Three Kings
We three kings of Orient are;
bearing gifts we traverse afar,
field and fountain, moor and mountain,
following yonder star.

O star of wonder, star of light,
star with royal beauty bright,
westward leading, still proceeding,
guide us to thy perfect light.

Words and music: John H. Hopkins Jr., 1857

Scripture

When they saw that the star had stopped, they were
overwhelmed with joy. On entering the house, they saw
the child with Mary his mother; and they knelt and paid
him homage. Then, opening their treasure chests, they
offered him gifts of gold, frankincense, and myrrh. (Matt.
2:10-11)

Reflection

Today is Epiphany, the day we celebrate the coming of the
Magi. In the Hispanic world, it is known as "The Day of
the Three Kings" (*El Día de los Tres Reyes*). In many
Hispanic and Latin cultures this is the day when gifts are

given. The Eastern Orthodox Church celebrates January 6 as the date of Jesus' birth, the Epiphany of the Lord.

Buy a Kings' Cake from a local Hispanic bakery and hold a celebration with friends, coworkers, or family. Sing together Christmas carols that talk about the arrival of the Magi.

Read Matthew 2:1-12. Talk together about the gifts you would bring if you had followed the star to the stable of Bethlehem.

PRAYER

Star of wonder,
you have led us,
along with so many,
to the Child of the Light.
Continue to guide us on our journey
to be Followers of the One,
the Creator and Redeemer
and Sustainer of us all.
For it is in Christ's name
that we pray,
Amen.

GROUP *Study Guide*

FOR THE LEADER

The leader helps create a safe place for group members to travel this Advent and Christmas season as they reflect on how God is working in their individual lives. Before each weekly session, read over the outline for that week's group time as well as each day's readings. Be sure to gather any extra supplies or resources that will be needed in leading the group.

Order the books several weeks in advance of the first session, and make sure each participant has a copy. If group sessions are not held on Sunday, think about whether the first group gathering should be during the week preceding the first Sunday of Advent.

At the first session, lead the group in developing some common guidelines to create a safe place for your time together as a group. The sample guidelines below can be a starting place for your group. Be sure to adapt these to meet your group's needs.

GROUP GUIDELINES

The purpose of this group is to encourage and provide mutual support for our individual journeys through the Advent and Christmas seasons. We covenant to meet weekly during Advent and to come together one time between December 25 and January 6 for a final session. Further, we covenant together to read each day's meditation and to participate in reflection, journaling, and prayer.

Here are some group guidelines to help us make this a safe place for our group.

- The group will start and end on time.

- Members of the group covenant to be present at every session. However, if circumstances prevent someone from attending a session, that person will let the leader know. Members of the group can continue to support that person in his or her absence.

- We will respect what other people say. Group sharing is based on each person's experience. We will not give advice or try to fix another person. We honor other individuals' experiences by listening deeply rather than focusing on what we will say next.

- We will give others time to share. Being aware of the time when sharing assures others they have time also. We understand that sharing in the group is not mandatory. If someone does not wish to say anything, we respect that person's choice.

- We will honor group confidentiality. What people talk about in the group stays in the group.

Participants may want to share phone numbers or e-mail addresses to be in touch with one another for support during the coming weeks.

Don't be afraid of silence. If there are times when no one has anything to say, rest in the quiet. God may be speaking during that time of silence.

WEEK 1

Come, Thou Long-Expected Jesus

CENTERING

Sing together, read responsively, or listen to this week's hymn, "Come, Thou Long-Expected Jesus." Light the first candle of the Advent wreath or a single candle, reminding the group that God is present in this time together.

REFLECTING

Ask: How have we seen, heard, or experienced God working in our lives or in the world today? in the past week?

READING SCRIPTURE

Read Isaiah 40:3-5.

GOING DEEPER

Read aloud the first section on pages 9–10 from "A Coming into Being."

What challenges do we face as we enter this Advent season of waiting and preparation? How is God calling us during this Advent to "come into being"?

CLOSING

Ask participants if they would like to share any prayer concerns. Close with a time of prayer or use the prayer from Monday (p. 20).

WEEK 2

I Want to Walk as a Child of the Light

CENTERING

Sing together, read responsively, or listen to this week's hymn, "I Want to Walk as a Child of the Light." Light the first two candles of the Advent wreath or a single candle, reminding the group that God is present in this time together.

REFLECTING

Ask: How have we seen, heard, or experienced God working in our lives or in the world today? in the past week?

With which meditation did individuals most connect during this week? What thought, reflection, or practice presented difficulty?

READING SCRIPTURE

Read Isaiah 9:2.

GOING DEEPER

Reflect on the presence of God's light through the promised coming of the Christ. Ask: What places need to be touched by God's light? What situations especially need God's comfort, healing, and peace? in the world, in your community, in your family, or in your individual life?

Share reflections as persons are able. After group members have had a chance to share their thoughts, read the following text responsively.

Leader: The people who walked in darkness have seen a great light; those who lived in a land of deep darkness—on them light has shined.
Group: Shine your light, O God, on our world and our community.
Leader: Shine your light, O God, on our families and in our relationships.
Group: Shine your light, O God, into the corners of our hearts.
Leader: Shine your light, O God, that we might reflect your brightness to all that we meet.
Group: And the people said, Amen.

CLOSING

Ask participants if they would like to share any prayer concerns. Close with a time of prayer or use the prayer from Friday (p. 45).

WEEK 3

O Come, O Come, Emmanuel

CENTERING

Sing together, read responsively, or listen to this week's hymn, "O Come, O Come, Emmanuel." Light the first three candles of the Advent wreath or a single candle, reminding the group that God is present in this time together.

REFLECTING

Ask: How have we seen, heard, or experienced God working in our lives or in the world today? in the past week?

With which meditation did individuals most connect during this week? What thought, reflection, or practice presented difficulty?

READING SCRIPTURE

Read Matthew 1:18-25.

GOING DEEPER

The name *Emmanuel* means "God is with us." Read or sing together the refrain from this week's hymn. "Rejoice! Rejoice! Emmanuel shall come to thee, O Israel."

We each are Israel, to whom Emmanuel is coming. Read or sing the refrain together again, using these words, "Rejoice! Rejoice! Emmanuel shall come to *me*, O Israel."

Ask: What does it mean to you that Emmanuel comes to you? Ask what feelings or thoughts this message evokes among the group members. Share these thoughts or feelings as persons are comfortable.

At the end of the sharing time, read or sing together the hymn, using whatever version of the refrain people prefer.

CLOSING

Ask participants if they would like to share any prayer concerns. Close with a time of prayer or use the prayer from Tuesday (p. 55).

WEEK 4

Lo, How a Rose E'er Blooming

CENTERING

Sing together, read responsively, or listen to this week's hymn, "Lo, How a Rose E'er Blooming." Light all four candles of the Advent wreath or a single candle, reminding the group that God is present in this time together.

REFLECTING

Ask: How have we seen, heard, or experienced God working in our lives or in the world today? in the past week?

With which meditation did individuals most connect during this week? What thought, reflection, or practice presented difficulty?

Reading Scripture

Read Luke 1:46-55.

Going Deeper

We are in the fourth week of Advent, the last week of preparation before Christmas. What are members experiencing as they try to maintain a sense of preparation and waiting (Advent themes) rather than celebration (Christmas themes)?

This week's meditations focus on Mary's Magnificat. Through this prayer Mary models the spiritual disciplines of listening, trusting, believing, waiting, and praising. Consider ways that we participate in these spiritual disciplines in our lives. Which are our strongest disciplines? Which need further nurture and development?

Ask each person to pick one of these spiritual disciplines to hold in awareness during the next few days. Share with one another the discipline you will be nurturing in this way. Encourage each other through prayer during these final days of Advent.

Closing

Ask participants if they would like to share any prayer concerns. Close with a time of prayer or use the prayer from Thursday (p. 76).

Week 5

What Child Is This?, Away in a Manger, and Other Christmas Favorites

CENTERING

Sing together, read responsively, or listen to one or more or this week's hymns. (Let the group pick their favorites to sing.) Light the four Advent candles and the Christ Candle or a single candle, reminding the group that God is present in this time together.

REFLECTING

Ask: How have we seen, heard, or experienced God working in our lives or in the world today? in the past week?

With which meditation did individuals most connect during this week? What thought, reflection, or practice presented difficulty?

READING SCRIPTURE

Read Psalm 98.

GOING DEEPER

Reflect on the spiritual journey during the Advent and Christmas seasons.

What have been the most meaningful moments in individual, family, or group time?

Reflect on individual journeys during this time. What

have been the surprises? What have been the challenges? What are the ways that people are singing "new songs" to God? What practices or disciplines would individuals like to take into the coming year? Share these reflections as each person feels led.

CLOSING

If you have time before the closing prayer, sing or read together more favorite Christmas hymns. Ask participants if they would like to share any prayer concerns. Close with a time of prayer and a sending forth into the world (or use the prayer from January 6, p. 101.)

About the Author

BETH A. RICHARDSON is an ordained deacon in the Tennessee Conference of The United Methodist Church. She currently serves as Director of Electronic Content at Upper Room Ministries (upperroom.org and MethodX.net) and as deacon at Edgehill United Methodist Church. Beth received her Master of Divinity from Vanderbilt Divinity School in Nashville, Tennessee. Beth grew up in Oklahoma and has always used music in her ministry. She has contributed her writing to *Alive Now* magazine, *The Upper Room Disciplines*, and two volumes of *The Storyteller's Companion to the Bible*.